ASK ISAAC ASIMOV ?

How is paper made?

Heinemann

First published in Great Britain by Heinemann Library
an imprint of Heinemann Publishers (Oxford) Ltd
Halley Court, Jordan Hill, Oxford OX2 8EJ

OXFORD LONDON EDINBURGH MADRID
ATHENS BOLOGNA PARIS MELBOURNE
SYDNEY AUCKLAND SINGAPORE TOKYO
IBADAN NAIROBI HARARE GABORONE
PORTSMOUTH NH (USA)

98 97 96 95 94

10 9 8 7 6 5 4 3 2 1

British Library Cataloguing in Publication Data is available from the British Library on request.

ISBN 0 431 07647 2

Cover designed and pages typeset by Philip Parkhouse
Printed in China

Picture Credits
pp. 2-3, © D. Muench/H. Armstrong Roberts; pp. 4-5, © Ken Novak, 1992; pp. 6-7, © E. R. Degginger/Picture
Perfect USA; p. 6 (inset), © Mary Evans Picture Library; pp. 8-9, © D. Muench/H. Armstrong Roberts;
p. 8 (inset), © Norman Tomalin/Bruce Coleman Limited; pp. 10-11, © John Zoiner; pp. 12-13, © John Zoiner;
pp. 14-15, Kurt Carloni/Artisan, 1992; pp. 16-17, © John Coster-Mullen/Third Coast Stock Source; pp.
18-19, © Bruce Paton/Panos Pictures; p. 19 (inset), © J. Hartley/Panos Pictures; pp. 20-21, © W. Metzen/
H. Armstrong Roberts; pp. 22-23, © D. Muench/H. Armstrong Roberts; p. 24, © D. Muench/H. Armstrong
Roberts

Cover photograph © Spectrum Colour Library
Back cover photograph © Sygma/D. Kirkland

The book designer wishes to thank the models for their helpful cooperation.

Series editor: Valerie Weber
Editors: Barbara J. Behm and Patricia Lantier-Sampon
Series designer: Sabine Beaupré
Book designer: Kristi Ludwig
Picture researcher: Diane Laska

Contents

Words that appear in the glossary are printed in **bold** the first time they occur in the text.

Modern-day wonders

Pick up your telephone and talk to someone halfway round the world. Press a few buttons on a microwave oven and have a hot meal in seconds. These are only some of the many wonders of technology.

One of today's most useful products is paper. Without paper, we would have no books, newspapers or letters from friends. Businesses would grind to a halt. How is paper made? Let's find out.

Who made papyrus?

Along the banks of the River Nile in Egypt, reeds wave gently in the breeze. These simple plants were very important in ancient times. The Egyptians slit open the reeds, scraped out the inner fibres and pressed the fibres together. The result was **papyrus**, a material on which the Egyptians wrote their important records. Papyrus scrolls have survived for more than 4000 years. Papyrus is thicker than paper. The Chinese people first made paper around AD 100.

What is paper made of?

Tear off a corner of a piece of paper and look at the torn edge with a magnifying glass. Notice the tiny fibres that stick out from the paper's edge. These fibres come from plants. They are the main ingredient in paper.

Paper used to be made from scraps of cotton and linen. In the early 1800s, the demand for paper outgrew the supply of scrap cloth. People began making paper out of ground-up wood mixed with water. This mixture is called wood pulp.

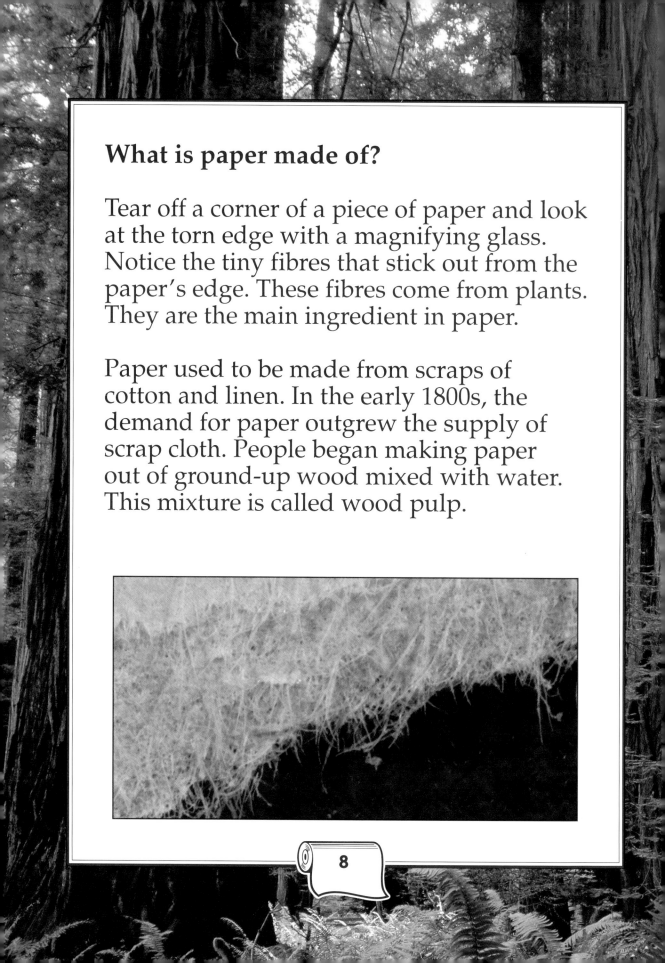

How is wood pulp made?

There are two ways to make wood pulp. One way is to take the bark off logs, soak the logs in water and grind them into tiny pieces. This is called the **mechanical** method.

The second method is called the **chemical** method. With this method, wood chips are soaked in chemicals and cooked over a high heat. The heat and the chemicals dissolve a substance called lignin. This is the natural glue that holds wood fibres together.

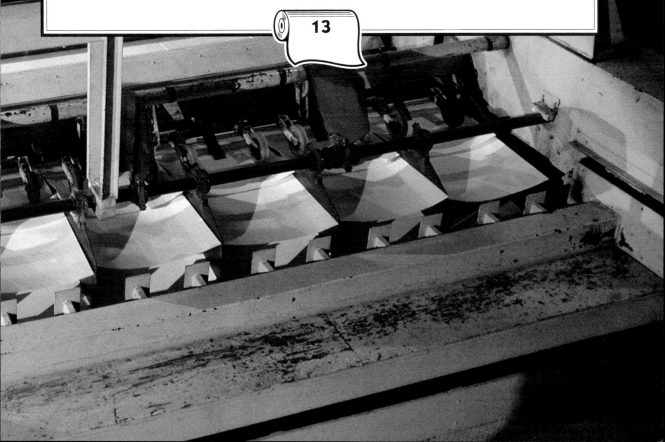

How is wood pulp processed?

Wood pulp is washed and pushed through a screen to remove the fibres too large for making paper. Next, the smaller fibres are bleached to make them white. Then different kinds of fibres are blended together. Fibres produced by the mechanical method are used in low-quality paper. Fibres produced by the chemical method are used in high-quality paper. These fibres do not contain lignin, which makes paper yellow with age. Most papers are made of a mixture of the two types of fibres.

How does pulp become paper?

The wood pulp, which is mostly water, is poured on to a huge, metal screen. Find this screen in the diagram below. The screen moves forward. Rollers press on the screen to remove most of the water. As the wood

14

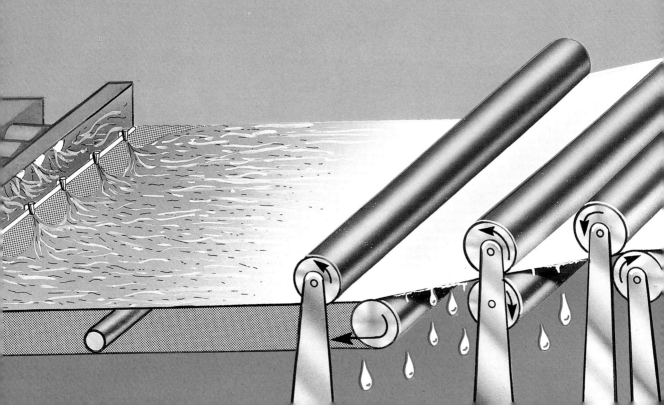

pulp dries, the fibres bond, forming a paper. Iron rollers, called the calender stack, smooth and polish the paper. Then the paper is wound on to large rolls. The paper stored on these rolls can be cut into smaller sheets.

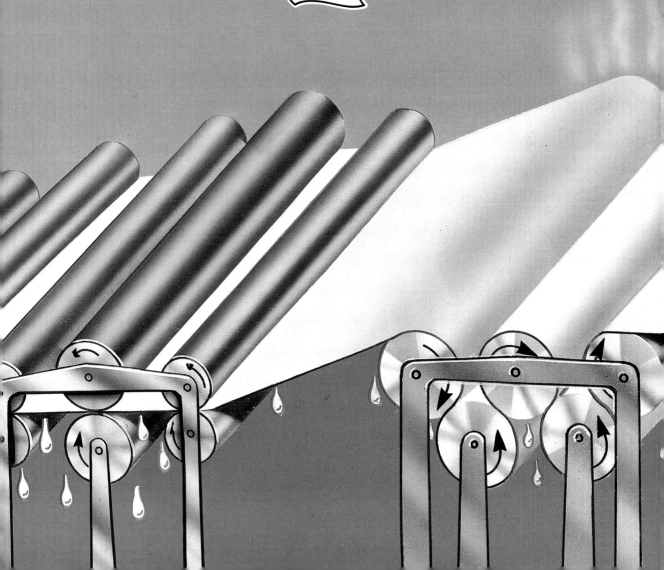

Can paper be recycled?

Making wood pulp into paper does not destroy the fibres. They can be used again, and so paper itself can be **recycled**. Recycling paper involves collecting used paper, sorting it out according to colour and quality, and cleaning it to remove staples or other non-paper items. Then the clean, sorted paper is wetted and beaten to loosen the fibres. The recycled fibres can be made into cardboard or newsprint, or mixed with wood pulp to make higher-quality paper.

16

Destroying forests for the trees

Vast numbers of trees are cut down for paper-making. Trees are a **renewable** resource: if some are cut down, others can be planted. But **clear-cutting**, removing all the trees in an area, makes the soil wash away, so trees cannot grow back. Even if new trees are planted, the forest and its inhabitants may die off. If only one type of tree is replanted, animals needing other types of trees for food or shelter can no longer live in the forest.

Can paper-making cause pollution?

The destruction of forests is not the only problem our hunger for paper causes. Making paper also causes pollution. Most paper companies use **chlorine** to bleach wood pulp. Chlorine mixes with other

chemicals that dissolve out of the wood, forming **dioxins**. Dioxins are chemicals that can cause cancer. Waste water from most paper companies contains these harmful chemicals. The water, polluted with dioxins, is dumped into lakes and rivers. Fish from the polluted waters are unsafe to eat.

How can we solve the paper problem?

Think of all the ways you use paper. The list is almost endless! But too much of a good thing can cause problems. We can help solve the paper problem by buying unpackaged goods whenever possible, recycling paper and asking paper-makers to stop using chlorine in their paper-making process.

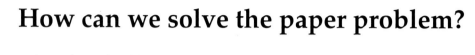

22

Glossary

chemicals: substances that make up our world. Everything is made of chemicals. The chemical method of making wood pulp involves using heat and chemicals to break down wood chips.

chlorine: a chemical that is an active agent in bleaches or whiteners

clear-cutting: the logging practice of cutting down or removing all the trees in an area of a forest

dioxin: a harmful chemical that results when chlorine mixes with materials that dissolve out of wood

lignin: a natural glue in wood that holds the fibres together

mechanical: relating to a machine. The mechanical method of making wood pulp involves grinding logs without bark in water.

papyrus: an ancient Egyptian writing material made from the inner fibres of reeds

recycle: to reuse a material by cleaning it and recovering the useful elements

renewable: capable of being replaced by natural processes

Index